Rosh Hashanah

Coloring Book
For Kids!

Belongs To:

D1227994

L'SHANAH
TOVAH!

Title:Rosh Hashanah Coloring Book For Kids

Author:Naomi Rover School

ISBN:9798530115493

TEST COLOR PAGE

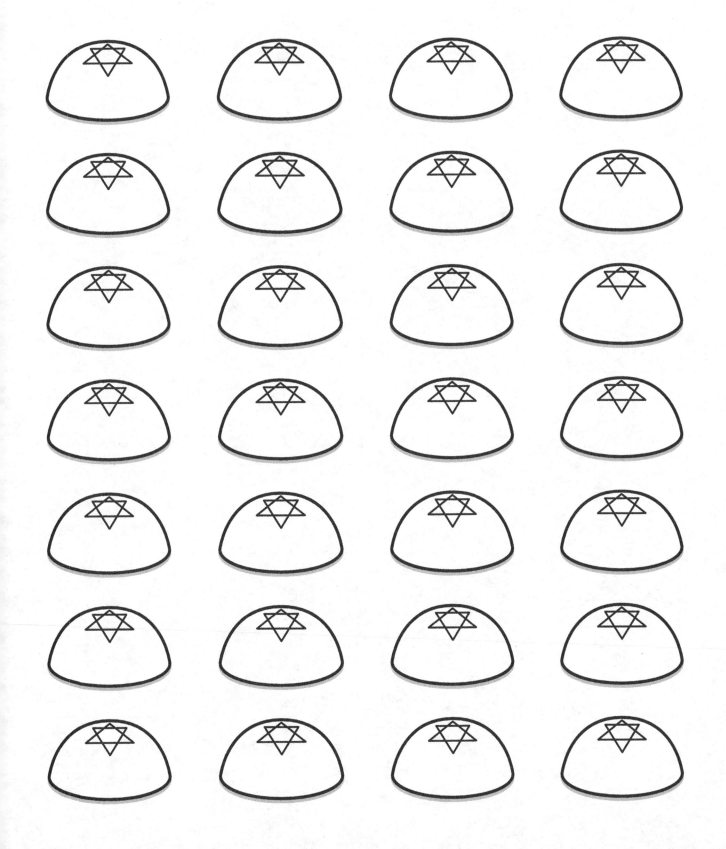

Single-sided pages - every image is placed on its own black-backed page
to reduce the bleed-through problem found in other coloring books

L'SHANAH TOVAH!

APPLES

Single-sided pages - every image is placed on its own black-backed page
to reduce the bleed-through problem found in other coloring books

L'SHANAH TOVAH!

HONEY

Single-sided pages - every image is placed on its own black-backed page
to reduce the bleed-through problem found in other coloring books

L'SHANAH TOVAH!

BEE

L'SHANAH TOVAH!

MACHZOR

Single-sided pages - every image is placed on its own black-backed page
to reduce the bleed-through problem found in other coloring books

L'SHANAH TOVAH!

CHALLAH
BREAD

Single-sided pages - every image is placed on its own black-backed page
to reduce the bleed-through problem found in other coloring books

L'SHANAH TOVAH!

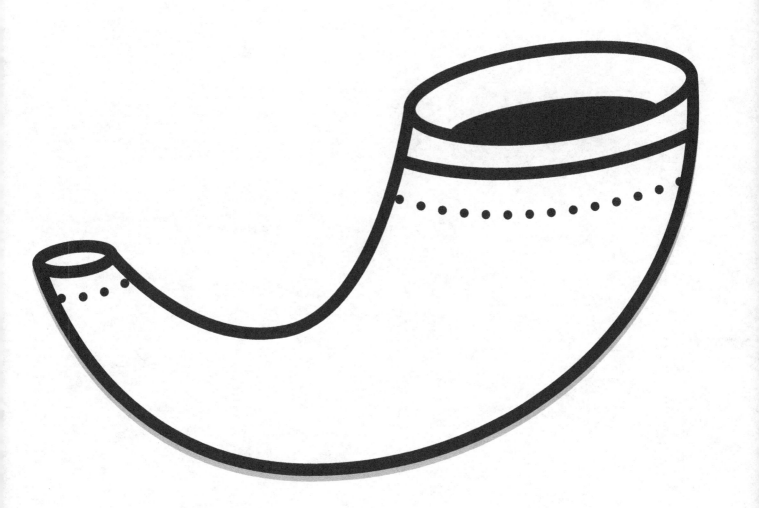

SHOFAR

Single-sided pages - every image is placed on its own black-backed page
to reduce the bleed-through problem found in other coloring books

L'SHANAH TOVAH!

WINE

Single-sided pages - every image is placed on its own black-backed page
to reduce the bleed-through problem found in other coloring books

L'SHANAH TOVAH!

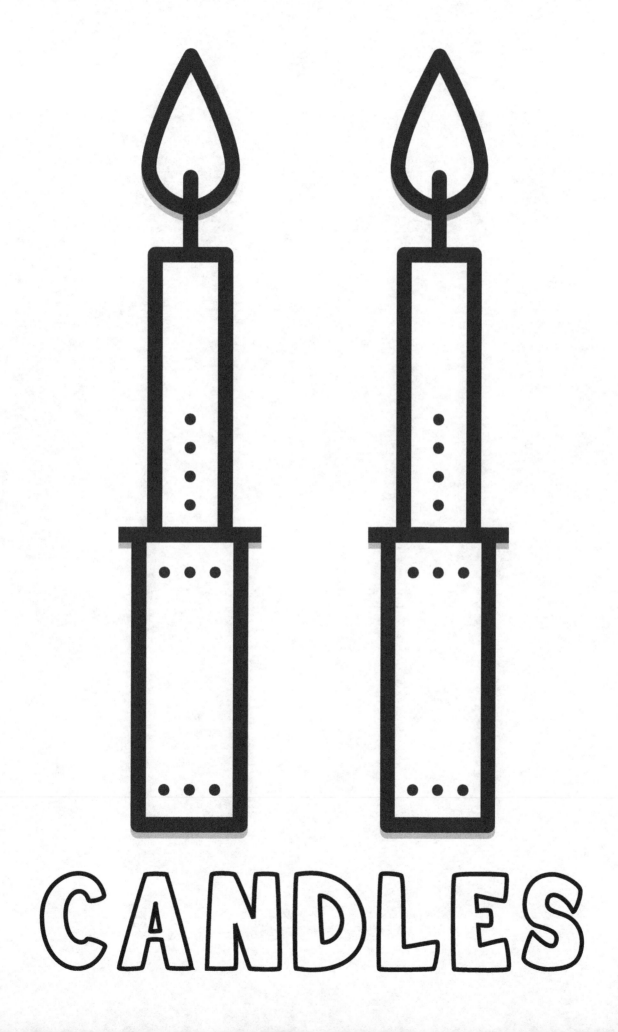

CANDLES

Single-sided pages - every image is placed on its own black-backed page
to reduce the bleed-through problem found in other coloring books

L'SHANAH TOVAH!

SHANAH TOVAH

Single-sided pages - every image is placed on its own black-backed page
to reduce the bleed-through problem found in other coloring books

L'SHANAH TOVAH!

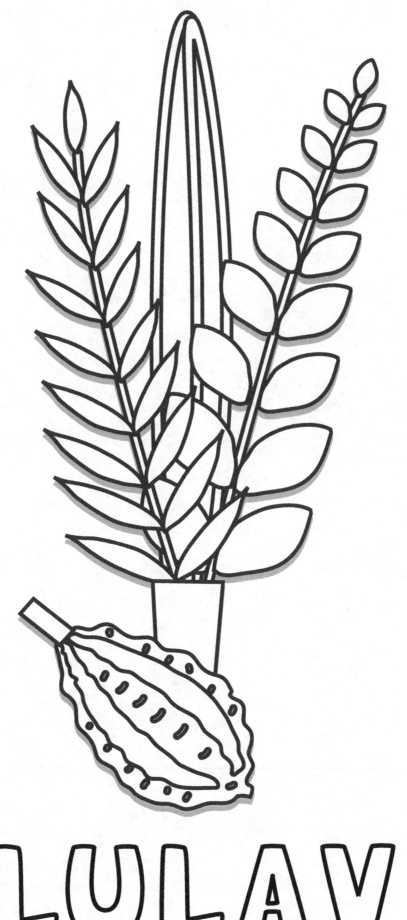

LULAV

Single-sided pages - every image is placed on its own black-backed page
to reduce the bleed-through problem found in other coloring books

L'SHANAH TOVAH!

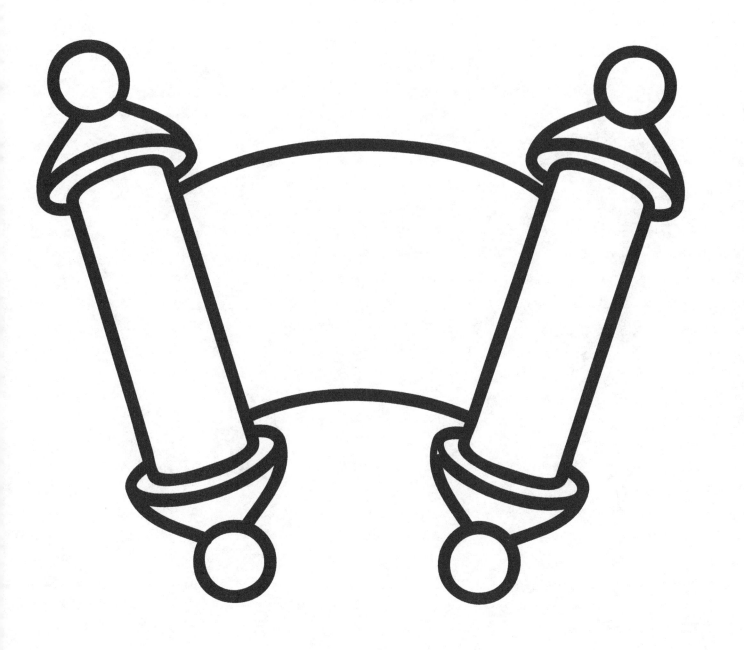

TORAH

Single-sided pages - every image is placed on its own black-backed page
to reduce the bleed-through problem found in other coloring books

L'SHANAH TOVAH!

FISH

Single-sided pages - every image is placed on its own black-backed page
to reduce the bleed-through problem found in other coloring books

L'SHANAH TOVAH!

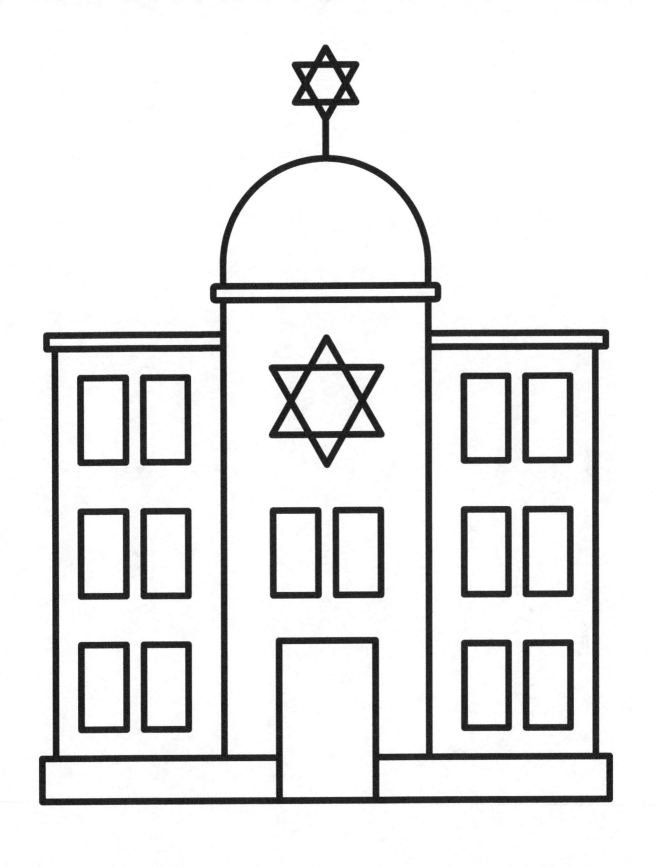

SYNAGOGUE

Single-sided pages - every image is placed on its own black-backed page
to reduce the bleed-through problem found in other coloring books

L'SHANAH TOVAH!

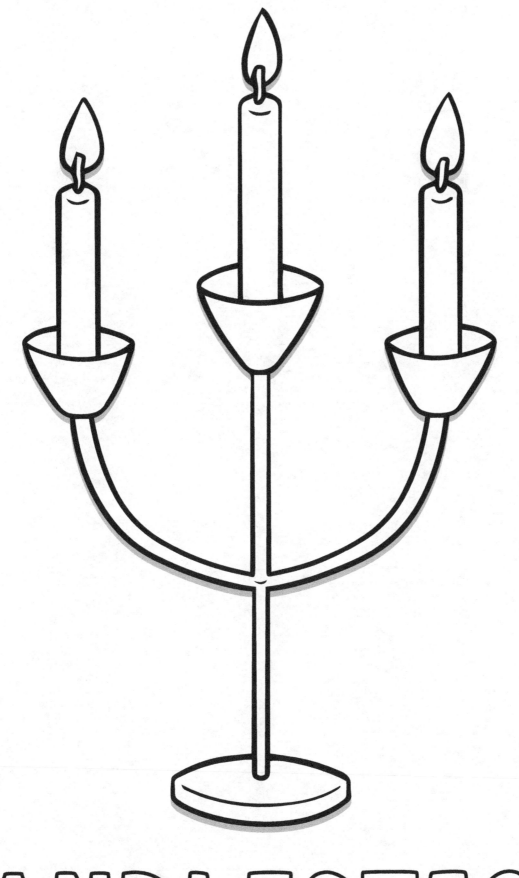

CANDLESTICK

Single-sided pages - every image is placed on its own black-backed page
to reduce the bleed-through problem found in other coloring books

L'SHANAH TOVAH!

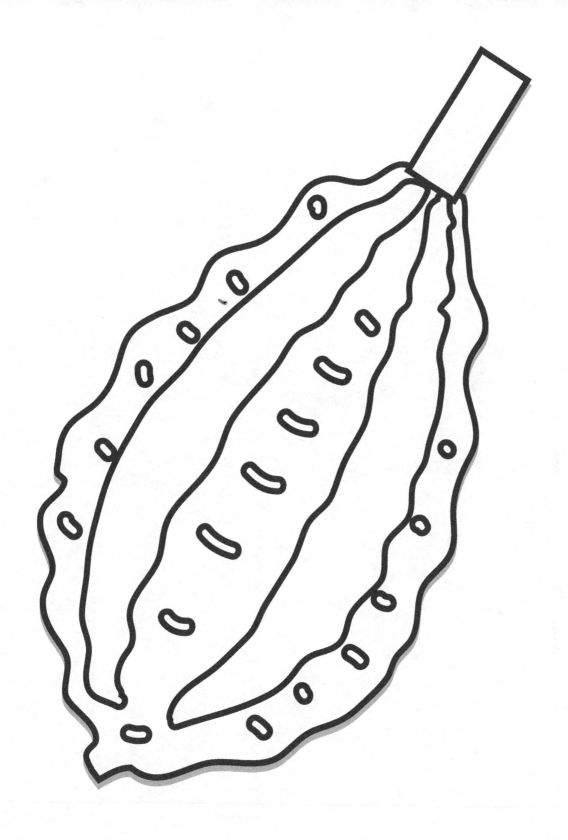

ETROG

Single-sided pages - every image is placed on its own black-backed page
to reduce the bleed-through problem found in other coloring books

L'SHANAH TOVAH!

BREAD
CRUMBS

Single-sided pages - every image is placed on its own black-backed page
to reduce the bleed-through problem found in other coloring books

L'SHANAH TOVAH!

POMEGRANATE

Single-sided pages - every image is placed on its own black-backed page
to reduce the bleed-through problem found in other coloring books

L'SHANAH TOVAH!

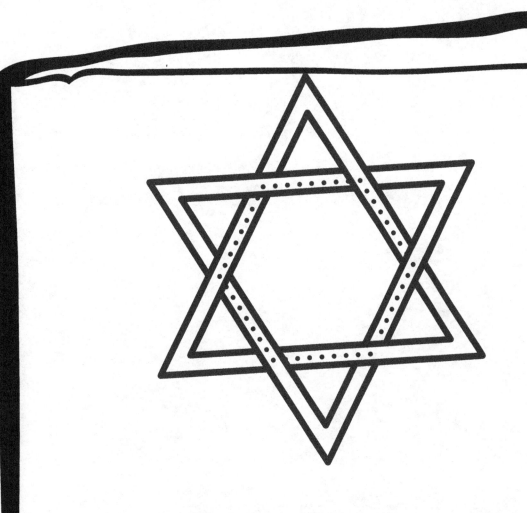

L'SHANAH
TOVAH!

GREETING
CARD

Single-sided pages - every image is placed on its own black-backed page
to reduce the bleed-through problem found in other coloring books

L'SHANAH TOVAH!

I AM VERY GRATEFUL FOR PURCHASING THIS BOOK. I HOPE YOU WILL SPEND AN UNFORGETTABLE TIME WITH YOUR CHILD, HAVING FUN AND LEARNING FROM THIS BOOK

IF IT WOULD NOT BE A PROBLEM FOR YOU I WOULD BE EXTREMELY GRATEFUL FOR LEAVING A REVIEW ON AMAZON. WE ARE A SMALL FAMILY BUSINESS AND THROUGH REVIEWS, WE CAN REACH MORE PEOPLE.

THANK YOU AGAIN FOR YOUR PURCHASE AND YOUR TRUST. I WISH YOU ENJOY YOUR BOOK AND HAVE A GREAT TIME WITH YOUR FAMILY

L'SHANAH TOVAH!

WE HOPE THE BOOK HAS MET YOUR EXPECTATIONS, IF YOU FOUND ANY MISTAKES IN THE BOOK PLEASE CONTACT US BY EMAIL, AND WE WILL CORRECT THEM AS SOON AS POSSIBLE.

office.dannyd@gmail.com

ROSH HASHANAH

INDEPENDENTLY PUBLISHED
Naomi Rover School

ILLUSTRATIONS:
SHUTTERSTOCK

Made in the USA
Monee, IL
26 August 2022

12638067R00024